Beyond Freedom

TALKS WITH
SRI NISARGADATTA MAHARAJ

D1591154

Edited by
Maria Jory

YogiImpressions®

YogiImpressions®

BEYOND FREEDOM
First published in India in 2007 by
Yogi Impressions Books Pvt. Ltd.
1711, Centre 1, World Trade Centre,
Cuffe Parade, Mumbai 400 005, India.
Website: www.yogiimpressions.com

First Edition, August 2007
Fourth reprint: September 2016

Copyright © 2007 by S. K. Mullarpattan

ISBN 978-81-88479-53-5

Printed at: Repro India Ltd., Mumbai

I talked to Maurice Frydman some four years back and he edited my words, emphasizing certain points and adding his own ideas, in the book 'I Am That'. That book and whatever was expounded at that time was only relevant for that period. I am speaking differently today. As a matter of fact, this should also have been recorded and published as it is in greater detail, and is emphasizing different aspects.

— Sri Nisargadatta Maharaj

Contents

Editor's Note

The wisdom teachings of the legendary sage Sri Nisargadatta Maharaj, have had the greatest impact on my life perspective. I can only read a couple of paragraphs of his teachings at a time and then find myself in stillness unable to read further.

I have never failed to marvel at the way the 'cosmic plan' unfolds, regardless, perfectly as always, despite us, and also at the many synchronicities and catalysts that often precede events. I had heard about Maharaj's interpreter and friend Saumitra Mullarpattan and asked around for his contact details with no success. Life has taught me that when situations are blocked, to stop forcing the jigsaw to fit, as when it is meant to fall into place, life unfolds spontaneously and effortlessly. In this case, however, I gave it one more try and visited my dear friends Chaitan Balsekar and his beautiful wife Neela to ask if they could help. Chaitan, who is always supportive, telephoned Mullarpattan who was his friend and I was invited to afternoon tea that same day.

A couple of days later I was having a conversation with a publisher, Gautam Sachdeva, before *satsang* with Ramesh Balsekar, who had also been an interpreter of Maharaj. We simultaneously had the idea of putting together a book about Maharaj. I mentioned our plan to Mullarpattan and he generously gave us ten recorded tapes of Sri Nisargadatta Maharaj's talks with seekers during the last two years of his life.

The tapes were full of the 'sounds of India'. It was difficult to hear what was being spoken in between the noise of the traffic, loud music, dogs barking, and carpentry work, not forgetting to mention the various birds competing with each other to be heard, also at *satsang* with Maharaj! I do not understand Marathi, yet it was deeply invigorating to hear the passion and energy with which Maharaj spoke on the tapes and strangely enough, on occasions, even understood what he was saying!

Mullarpattan had done a marvellous job of interpreting Maharaj's words. It must have been a daunting task, as he often spoke for some length of time before the interpreter was able to translate. It would have been impossible for him to translate word for word of what had been spoken. I therefore had to find a person who understood Marathi, who could give me a literal translation of what Maharaj had said on the tapes. Once again, I discussed my dilemma with Chaitan and Neela Balsekar and discovered to my delight and relief that Neela was fluent in Marathi and was happy, together with Chaitan, to help with the literal translation of the tapes.

Transcribing and editing this book has been the greatest joy. Refining the chapters, daily, over so many months, hammered Maharaj's concepts relentlessly, deeper and deeper, until they have now become part of the fabric of my being. My sincere wish in editing this book was to represent accurately, as much as editorially possible, the precise words of Maharaj during his talks. I retained what some may consider to be 'poor English' in order to preserve the distinctive way that Maharaj expressed himself. I was aware that much could be lost by overzealous editing. It was heartening to hear a comment by my daughter that she did not see any of my style of writing in the editing of this book.

The photo-painting of Maharaj reproduced on the cover of this book was created by my artist friends Trevor and Tim Gainey. When I told them it was to be included, they replied, *"They were happy that others would be able to experience their work as it had been such a powerful experience painting it."* I offer them my heartfelt appreciation for their awesome picture.

I would like to thank Saumitra Mullarpattan for his kindness in giving us the material for this book and for his generous hospitality during my visits to his home.

I also thank Gautam Sachdeva of *Yogi Impressions* for his support and encouragement during the process of editing this book.

I especially thank Chaitan Balsekar and his wife Neela, for their friendship, support and invaluable translations, without which this book would never have been published.

Many thanks also to my daughter Racquel who proof-read the edited scripts and encouraged me all the way as she has always done.

Lastly, I offer my sincere gratitude to Sri Nisargadatta Maharaj for using this body-mind as a vehicle to incorporate the tapes of his talks and teachings in print. Because of this, everyone who reads this book has been given the life changing opportunity to experience the flavour and essence of this great Master.

– Maria Jory
October 2006

Foreword

When I look back at the series of events that led to the publication of this book, it is a reconfirmation that what the Source has ordained must come to pass.

Last year when I discovered, quite by chance, that the *samadhi* of the guru of Sri Nisargadatta Maharaj was in the vicinity of my residence in South Mumbai, I decided to visit it that weekend. I was quite astonished to find that the *samadhi* was at the Banganga cremation grounds. But then, the thought occurred to me that there really was no better place than this – to which Maharaj's teaching that "you are not your body" could have brought me. A feeling of peace and calm pervaded the place, as a gentle breeze floated up from the sea.

Seated near the *samadhi* was an old man. I struck up a conversation with him and learned that he had, on several occasions, sat in the *satsangs* of Maharaj. I asked whether he was aware if there were any talks of Maharaj that had not been published so far, as there must have been a number of recordings made during those years. He answered that he had no clue, but there was one person, called Mullarpattan, who might know something about it. Unfortunately, he did not have any address or contact number of this person. So I left it at that, but with the thought that if there were more tapes, it would be a great idea to bring them out in the form of a book.

The following Sunday, I was waiting below Ramesh Balsekar's (a disciple of Maharaj) apartment before the start of the morning *satsangs* at his residence. It was there that I met Maria Jory. We spoke casually and she asked me what I had been up to of late. I mentioned that I had recently visited the *samadhi* of Sri Nisargadatta Maharaj's guru, and now I was looking for a person by the name of Mullarpattan. I can still recall the surprised look on Maria's face as I uttered that name. She exclaimed that she was, quite coincidentally, meeting him that very evening! She told me that Mullarpattan had been Maharaj's translator for the longest period of time.

She invited me to come along with her to meet Mullarpattan that evening. We were greeted by a gracious, hospitable, and a very vibrant, ninety-one year-old man. Without much ado, Maria and I asked him if there were any tapes that had not yet been transcribed into a book, as they could be of enormous value for those interested in Maharaj's teachings. He kept reiterating that Maharaj used to say to "forget all books and go within."

On a subsequent visit, we were pleasantly surprised when he handed us a box of ten tapes. These tapes, later transcribed by Maria, form the book you now hold in your hands.

My heartfelt thanks go to Mullarpattan for presenting and entrusting us with this treasure of Maharaj's talks that had been lying forgotten for so long. This now gives seekers a rare opportunity to get a further taste of Maharaj's teachings. To Maria, for all the hard work she has put in and for her patience with this project. To Chaitan and Neela Balsekar, for their help in translating the Marathi spoken by Nisargadatta Maharaj. And especially to Gary Roba, for his invaluable contribution in patiently going through the teaching, over and over again, with a fine toothcomb and ironing out the rough edges.

I always thought of Maharaj's teachings as golden arrows going straight into the heart. When I mentioned this to a friend, he said, "Really? It was more like Maharaj was pumping bullets into me!"

It is our hope that this book impacts you in some way or another.

– Gautam Sachdeva
May 2007

What is That which you are searching for?

Maharaj: There is no sense of personality at all when you become the *Ishwara* principle. Have no concern about losing your personality by listening to this knowledge, as personality has always been illusory. In order to even understand me the sense of personality must be absent. You *are* the knowledge and you don't have any shape or form whatsoever. You are impersonal. You are comprehensive. You are the unmanifest, the Universal Consciousness. What would happen if you went in search of that Consciousness? The seeker would disappear in the search, because the "I Amness" is all there is.

Visitor: I have a question here.

M: Do not focus on your question. Focus on what I am saying. Don't say anything, just listen.

V: I am able to appreciate listening to you, therefore I am speaking.

M: Just leave the question, be strong.

V: You speak very harshly... it hurts me.

M: Just leave that. Do not even look in that direction, just focus on what I am telling you.

V: There was a split between what was there before the question and what came after.

M: Look at what was there before the question came up. Do not speak about what came after the question.

V: But I do not know who I am, that is my reality.

M: As long as you are coming here, your search is not over. You are here because the search has not ended. Try to find out why. What is That which you are searching for? There is nothing there, only the process of seeking.

You might be anybody in this world, even *Brahma* or *Vishnu,* but you do not have the power to do anything. Your life is your existence. It is made up of the five elements and it is dependent only on these five elements.

Consciousness is an orphan without parents or source. It has no need of anyone. What you understand of the objective world is all duality. Your objective world is composed of relationships. You have to depend all the time on someone else – friend, husband, wife, etc. In the objective world there is only dependence, whereas in your true state there is always independence. Existence without identity, which is your true nature, is independent. The time is half-past eleven at present, it cannot be twelve now. It will be twelve half an hour later. We don't have any control over it; the time has to pass. That means you are always dependent on something. You cannot live independently of time, space, or the elements. Everyone is helpless. Only Consciousness is independent.

The state of bliss or joy is *Poornabrahman* or *Nirvana*. One who does not need anybody for entertainment is *niranjan*. The ever-present is *nitya*. That state never changes at all. As long as you are conscious of your body and its needs, you cannot be totally independent. Consciousness does not need light and it does not need darkness. It does not need rest. It is the Truth and there is no change in it.

When I was young, I had the power to squeeze a piece of metal and pull it back into shape. Now I am old and require help from somebody to move around. Where has the power gone? It has not remained with me at all.

All of these things in the objective world are inseparable from their attributes. An attribute by its very nature depends upon something. That knowledge, "I Am," is also an attribute.

Therefore, the "I Amness," one way or another, also has to depend on something.

V: What is the concept of maya (illusion)?

M: The concept of *maya* comes from the "I Amness." The existence of *maya* and the world around you only arises when you are conscious of yourself. This is a state of darkness and ignorance, which is far from that of knowledge. *Maya* does not exist within the state of knowledge.

V: What is Atma Prem (Self-love)?

M: *Atma Prem* is also due to the "I Amness." If you start with *Atma Prem*, it can distract you and all you will see is *maya*, which is a state of ignorance. If you reach a state of knowledge, then even this *Atma Prem* will be non-existent. The word *maya* has a different meaning here. What you are calling love is itself *maya*. Love is playing many roles. All these houses, etc. have been created out of *maya*. Love or *maya* has set up the whole of Bombay. Love is taking many shapes; *mula-maya* has created *Vishnu* and *Shankara*, but what was there before that? *Maya* is the culprit. Man has entangled himself in this concept and illusion of love, and because of it gets trapped in the cycle of life and death. The feeling of love is a great mistake if one gets entangled in it. There is love for so many things. The minute the illusion is created, the entanglement begins. By imagining male and female, you got entangled in that illusion.

"You are the Paramatma." This is what my Guru told me when he was going into *Mahasamadhi*. His words had so much force that they were implanted and embedded in me, and I became That. There was so much power and force behind his utterances that whatever he said came true.

V: Were you constantly doing the sacred mantra, which your Guru had given you?

M: I was not doing it. I was constantly listening to it. The power of the *mantra* depends upon the intensity of the faith you have.

V: Is there any cause for this faith?

M: Yes, there is a primary cause, the big cause, which is the knowledge "I Am." This is the cause behind the faith. The 'Awareness of my Being' happened automatically. It just happens. The sprouting of this knowledge "I Am" is prior to the formation of the five elements. The Ultimate Consciousness, the Absolute, is not even aware of Itself or of any happening. Consciousness was One, but two people of different sexes were created and the love between them created this world. This sound and this awareness are not one, but two. Consciousness is just a speck, and this illusion has come out of it.

Love is divided into two sexes and the world has grown out of this, but as soon as realization happens this separation disappears. When you have the realization that 'You are', that all is the play of *Shiva Shakti*, then you will know that this is all an illusion, and you will be free of grief as well as joy. Self-realization is *Shivadatta*. The moment you reach that stage you will not have these feelings of happiness, sorrow and suffering. When you reach the state of Self-knowledge, there will be peace and quiet. Such knowledge of the Self is known as *Shivadatta*. If you realize that this is all an illusion, then there is no need for Self-realization.

V: Is there no love with Self-realization?

M: It is beyond that. Love is a worldly state. The very feeling of Self-realization will not arrive until you understand what you are. If you understand the answer then this question about Self-realization will not arise. *Ananda*, the pleasure and bliss of Consciousness, will arise in you like an atomic explosion, and you will see how the whole wide world is a manifestation of That. *Chinmayananda* means 'speck of bliss'. *Swami* means 'the spontaneous Awareness of my Being'. Through the "I Amness," Swami Chinmayananda has created a big ashram that many people visit. All the gods are coming and going in this Consciousness. Merely the fact that 'You are' is *Swami*, which is pure honey, the proof of the Absolute. It is always with you and has come all by itself spontaneously, without asking. That is *Swami*.

V: *And all the other things, what is all that about?*

M: Why worry about that? Let it be there. Worry about the "I Amness" and forget about the rest. What the *Swamis* are doing or what they say is immaterial. If you have come to the Source, why do you want to go back again to the banks of the river?

Knowledge of
your real identity

Maharaj: When the "I Amness" appears spontaneously, like a bolt of lightning, the illusion of Self-love is broken into five basic elements: space, air, earth, fire and water. But this Self-love, the "I Am," manifests as *Sattva Guna* to the one who accepts this as a natural process. When it is used for achieving something in the world, it is referred to as *Rajas Guna*. When it is used to take credit for achievements, it is referred to as *Tamas Guna*. All the elements merge into one, and through the earth they create the grass and the grain. Grass is the fodder for the animals that give us milk. Grain is the food of human beings, in which the subtlest principle is already embedded. When it is assimilated in the body, it becomes the 'food-body'. This food-body is formed out of the milk and the grains that we eat. When the vital force is there, the "I Amness" appears. "I Amness" is the *sattva* quality, which is from the word *sat* – to be. The "I Amness," which appears in a fraction of a second, is due to the food-body.

When an individual soul (*jiva*) is born, it becomes aware of its parents and then becomes aware of its pasture, grazing ground, and food. Shapes are formed according to their parent forms. A human being gives birth to a human being, animals give birth to animals, and snakes and worms are created from the lowest forms of life. Four-legged creatures and human beings are created from a higher life force. Self-love is unique to human beings. Everything is created from the 'seed'. When the parent form is mature, the seed is formed and the photo or form of the parent is stamped in the seed. Each seed creates an individual that is different from the others. The seed of one member of a family is quite different from that of his brother. The photograph in the seed is taken in a fraction of a second and the new creation is born according to the traditional form. Some species, like goats, are born after three months. Human beings are born after nine months.

All living beings, as well as every shape and form, are created from the merging of the five elements with the essence of the earth. There are four ways in which creation takes place. That which is created from the air, like bacteria and various insects, is referred to as *Udhvaja*. That which is born from water and the sweat of the body, like worms, etc. is referred to as *Svedaja*. That which is born from eggs, like snakes, fish, and birds, is referred to as *Undeja*. Animals and human beings, which have their own ways of procreating, are born from the earth element; this is referred to as *Jaraja*. Along with the five elements, a quality of the universe that is called destiny or *prarabdha* also comes into the formation. The process of birth does not arise through any deliberate action; it happens spontaneously. All actions are predetermined.

With so much 'mixing' going on now, I predict that all races will eventually blend together. Caste and creed will become meaningless and it will be impossible to identify a pure Indian or a pure European. The entire pattern of the human race will change. The divisions into Hindu, Muslim, or Christian will cease to exist. Male and female will be the only remaining categories.

As long as the identification with the body and the ego remains, you cannot be free. You will still just be following the same conventional pattern of behaviour as the rest of the world. But what is the genuine behaviour of your true *dharma*? With what identity are you asking me these questions? Your knowledge is the product of your perceived identity, but what knowledge do you have of your real identity? First understand that, before asking further questions.

What is it that you want most? What is it that you are running after? You love your body, and crave the things that give it pleasure. You feel egotistical pride for your achievements. But once you have found your real identity, that which 'You are', you will be stabilized in that Awareness. You will be free of greed, attachment, and pride. The thing which attracts you most of all is your "I Amness." You want to retain that "I Amness." You want to 'Be'. This "I Am" is what you truly love the most. You want to be alive.

Visitor: So, does the real freedom lie in being able to find out who you are?

M: When you discover that Self which has no colour, image, or design, you will no longer require freedom or be conditioned by freedom. You will be beyond freedom.

What is *yoga*? *Yoga* is uniting, two things joining together – that is *yoga*. The whole population is a result of *yoga*. One party mixing or joining together with the other produces offspring with the identity of both. Why do you seek *yoga*? *Yoga* means the bridge, the link, or the connection. Why are you seeking this connection? You have to find out why it has occurred. *Yoga* was not required prior to the appearance of the bridge. You must find out what your state was prior to the bridge. Whatever the principle or the state was before this linking, before the existence of the bridge, was the perfect state. Because the bridge has appeared you feel separated from your true Self, and you are trying to become reunited; that is *yoga*. Because of this, you have become the servant of your desires.

The method that the *yogis* practice is breath control. By controlling their breath, they are able to enter a state of *samadhi*. Because their desires have been suppressed for a time, they presume that they have attained Self-realization. Before meeting my Guru I had a liking for these things. Once, a great *yogi* came to visit. After controlling his breath, he'd allow a car or even a truck to run over him. This was the miraculous power that he could exhibit. But that was the scope of his *yogic* studies – control the breath, perform miracles and exhibit them. Those people who go into *samadhi* by holding their breath have only learned a skill. They do not have the knowledge, and they have not transcended the knowledge. With the acrobatics of breath they may temporarily achieve certain powers, but that is not real union with the Source. Knowledge of the Self (*jnana*) is required. They have not achieved Ultimate Unity with the Absolute.

The Awareness
of Presence

Maharaj: The meditation of focusing on the breath is known as *pranayama*. Doing *pranayama* gives you peace. However, the Witness is not the vital breath (*prana*) but the one who is watching without participating. It does not come from anywhere. It is always there. It is not fair or dark, and it is not square or round, or of any shape. You can call the One who is watching *Krishna*, Christ, or *Rama*. It is pure love. This Witness is each one's proof of his Being; this is 'the knowing'. What is this vital breath? When it is within you, in the body, it is called *prana*. When you meditate on the breath and when it is released, it merges with the atmosphere and becomes one with the universe. For this mode of worship you do not need any other materials, like food or flowers.

When you control your breath through *pranayama*, a state of bliss (*samadhi*) can be reached where there is no mind and therefore no desire. However, this state of bliss and happiness can only last as long as you maintain control of your breath. Soon, you will descend again to the gross state. It is only when this joy is beyond the senses that it merges with the universe. It is as pure as the sky, and like the sky it is infinite. But who gives it light? That love, that knowledge which gives it light, is the knowledge "I Am." Focus on your Beingness until you become established in it. Only then will you be able to transcend it. Your focus at present is only on air, or the breath. 'Be' that Beingness, though this is also not the final step.

Visitor: It does not matter what that experience is if you are aware of the Witness; am I correct?

M: Who is the Witness of this joy? Who is aware of this joy? Be that "I Am." Once you know who you are, remain stabilized in the experience of the Self. Be like Arjuna – Awareness of his Being remained with him constantly, even when he went into the thick of battle. Because he was one with *Krishna,* he could go into battle knowing that there is nobody who kills and no one who is killed.

V: There are so many difficult situations in spiritual practice like doing my sacred rituals, or controlling the breath. What do I do?

M: You don't do anything. First, you must take a vow or an oath that you are not a man.

V: How can I say that?

M: Why can't you? You can take an oath that you are not a human being. The knowledge that is prior to thought – "I Am" – is covered by a human body, which is lined with the vital breath and knowledge of the Self (*prana* and *jnana).* This means that you are only covered with a human body. Once you reach this state of "I Am" through your attention, you will only be aware of That, and you will no longer be affected by all of these tendencies (*vasanas*). You will have transcended them. Let your questions emanate from what you have just heard, and not from books or scriptures that you have read previously.

V: I only want some clarification about the knowledge of "I Am."

M: You have to be one with the Self, the "I Am." If you say 'knowledge', it is just the same as information. If necessary, discard the words "I Am." Even without the words you know that 'You are'. Do not say or even think that 'You are'. Just be aware of the Presence without thinking about it.

V: How do you know that you have reached the state of witnessing?

M: Who says that he is alive? Find out, who is the Witness who *knows* that he is alive? This is Awareness of one's existence, "I Am," prior to thought. Who says, "I am alive," who says, "I am not alive," what is that? "I Am" is not something that can be put into words; it is the knowledge, the Awareness before thought. You have to just 'Be'.

V: In me, at times, there is a continuous feeling, not thoughts, which I feel is 'I'.

M: All the religions of the world are based upon feeling and tradition. You can recite your *mantra* in whatever way you like. It is not going to make any difference because, as I have already told you, becoming stabilized in the Awareness "I Am" is all that is important. Later on, you will also transcend the "I Amness." What I am saying now is being recorded on a tape, but will I actually be talking when it is played back? No, it is only a chemical that was created by a human being. Similarly, there is a photograph of my Guru on the wall. Is it a real Guru? No. Man makes the picture with a chemical. In the same way, this human being created by God is also just a chemical, and you should be aware of that. Just as a storm is a form created by nature, similarly this "I Am," this chemical, was also created. Forget about what I have told you, because that is also a mechanical thing, a chemical. Just be Aware, and then it won't matter if you die a hundred times.

A dream world of which
You are the Source

Maharaj: Words are very powerful. If a man is told that he will die after three days, he is likely to believe it and will be concerned. Are you affected by the words being spoken to you now? Words can affect you and then disappear.

Visitor: A sage is not concerned whether his body is going to die or not.

M: Correct, but these are just parables.

V: You told us about the 'I'. I want to know who created the "I Am."

M: A child knows who created it. The parents are the creator of the child.

V: But the child does not know the birth of the parents.

M: These are all concepts. The child has been given an idea who its parents are, but it is just a concept. Similarly, the

"I Am" is just a concept. The child has also been given the idea that 'He is'. First you must investigate 'Who is', and what this "I Amness" is.

V: You talked about the "I Am." You construct an understanding that this "I Am" has to have a support.

M: You want to know what the support is for the "I Am?" My parents supported me! When do these two people, the husband and the wife, become parents? It's when a child is born; is that not true? Where are the parents before the birth of the child? And, what is that child? The child is the root of the parents. The child is also the father of the parents. Because of the child, the parents are. This shows how completely hollow our egos are. What is the use of this Beingness, when it is the Beingness that has determined all this play? Awareness is the Absolute, but who is the witness of the Absolute? The ego is like the child of a barren woman.

I am an uneducated person, yet people from all over the world come and visit me. What is this due to? It is because I have become a zero, a Nothingness. This knowledge has come spontaneously. Out of nothing, something 'is', and in that 'is-ness' or Beingness there are innumerable universes. But even this Beingness is discardable.

V: You say that your Consciousness has created this world. Does this mean that other people's Consciousness will create different worlds?

M: Yes, each person will create his own world or a different concept of the world. In your dream world there are so many people. Do the people in your dream world recognize that their world is born out of your Consciousness? So what type of great God can be born out of your Consciousness? Yet people pray to that Consciousness. Don't discuss what I have told you with all and sundry and don't expose it or you will be beaten with the pressure! This knowledge or understanding is only to be understood or observed. There is a couplet from Saint Tukaram: *"To begin with there is only one seed which sprouts and grows into a sapling, and then into a big tree. This tree will create many seeds which in turn will give birth to innumerable trees."*

V: My 'I' has created my world, and when I converse with other people I will talk to them about my world.

M: Yes, but does the other person know that you are talking to them about 'your' universe?

V: I do not know.

M: If you do not know, why are you asking the question? Take the example of a berry. One berry ripens, then falls and creates a new tree, which will bear many berries. These seeds will create a huge jungle. All of this is created from a single seed.

V: All of them had a single origin.

M: This is all a dream world of which *You* are the Source. If *You* do not exist, then the manifestation of the world will not be there for you. Do you realize that *You* have created your world?

V: I will try to understand.

M: There is no question of effort here. It has to be understood spontaneously.

V: What is the role I should play in this world?

M: Amongst all these millions of people, you are enquiring about your part in this world. What is the percentage of your contribution? By yourself you may be big, but in this crowd you are nobody.

V: What is my share in all this?

M: Go to Goenka's ashram, meditate a little more, and then maybe you will understand. I am only telling you my story, not that of *Brahma*. *Brahma* means illusion. Just like when deer run after a mirage in the hot sun, it is an illusion; the water is not really there. Similarly, you are running after illusions, thinking that something good will come out of it and that you will be blessed. But it is not true. This body is formed from food (*annamaya*) and is perishable. If the food-body were not there, the world would also not be there. Once the vital breath leaves the body and this "I Amness" ceases to exist, the "I Amness" will not know that 'It was'. The "I Amness" is not permanent and will forget its association with this body. Just as food is perishable, the body that is built from the nourishment of food is also perishable, and is not permanent.

If you have questions, ask the one who wants to know. Cling to the questioner – that is your own Beingness, or "I Amness." Once you've done that, people will also approach you. They will call you Mahatma, or Anandamayi. After this talk, will you remember at least one sentence of it clearly? When you're hungry and eat a meal, is it the first morsel or the last that satisfies you? I want you to answer this. This is the essence of all knowledge.

The words of the Guru
are Truth itself

Maharaj: When my Guru went into a state of bliss, He told me: *"Have faith in me and in my words. Whatever I am telling you is the Truth. You are the highest Truth. Have implicit faith in that and conduct yourself accordingly."*

There was a sage who was very temperamental, who got upset very easily. He used to curse with so much force and emphasis that whatever he said would take a concrete shape and happen. My Guru told me, *"Divinity (Paramatma) is what you are."* I heard it in the *satsang* (*sat* – true or wise, *sang* – association) of my Guru and I accepted it. I did not want to gain anything, I just accepted it. I never knew that 'I' existed and suddenly I was aware that "I Am" this Absolute Truth. I had complete faith in the words of my Guru, and then later on everything happened spontaneously. There was continuous transformation and I was astounded at what was happening in me. That was the strength of the words of my Guru. The words of the Guru are Truth itself.

Visitor: Were you constantly repeating the words which your Guru gave you?

M: I was always listening to that sacred recitation (*japa*), which was constantly happening inside me.

V: Is there any cause for this japa?

M: The primary cause is the knowledge that you have of "I Am".

V: What do you mean by 'knowledge'?

M: This knowledge of "I Am" spontaneously appeared. This knowledge of "I Am" is prior to the formation of the five elements. The Absolute (*Paramatma Parmeshwar*) is not aware of anything. The state of Awareness comes later, with the knowledge of the "I Am." A man may be well when he goes to sleep, but when he awakes in the morning he suddenly feels giddy and falls down. He discovers that his whole body is swollen, but he does not know the cause of his illness. Only when all the tests are done does he know the cause of his illness. Similarly, the Absolute had no knowledge that 'It was' (or that 'It is'). Only when the knowledge "I Am" spontaneously appeared could it be concluded that the Absolute 'was' or 'is'. It is only when the body-mind consciousness comes into existence, with the power of the five elements, that the Awareness arises. I was told by my Guru that this very principle that does not know that 'It is', is my Self. This is what was conveyed to me. It is from this standpoint that I am talking to you.

When I was young I used to ponder about many subjects. Before I met my Guru I used to think there was no such thing as spirituality. I took a vow that I would never get initiated or surrender to another person. One day a friend told me that a great sage was visiting the area and asked me to come along with him to meet the sage. I did not want to go but my friend encouraged me, so I went with him. My friend bought a garland and some sweets for the sage and suggested that I put on a nice suit for the visit. When I met the Guru, he asked me to close my eyes and he initiated me. After some time, the Guru asked me to open my eyes; it was as if I had exploded. From that moment on I was a different person.

In 1932, I purchased two books on philosophy that had been recommended by a friend. I tried to read them at the time but could not understand any of it, so I wrapped up the books and put them aside. My Guru initiated me in 1934. Within two months of the initiation that same friend took me to his village and suggested that we discuss those books on philosophy. I expounded the books spontaneously, which were to me, at this stage, like kindergarten information.

V: How did you acquire this ability?

M: This is like asking me how I acquired this human form without my knowledge! It just happened. I had no hand in it. People might praise me or run me down, but I was doing it without being aware of it, effortlessly and naturally. I had never studied the scriptures, yet the knowledge just came to me. It is said that there have been so many dissolutions of the universe, but how is it that 'I' am untouched by it? Actually, 'I' have always been there, only this present day form (body) may not have been there. Even the dissolution of the universe has not touched this 'I'.

This body has a shape, but 'I' as Consciousness do not have any shape. When you become habituated to carrying something with you it gets attached to you and you become one with it. If you eat a particular poison, grain by grain, you will become immune to it. Then, even a snake won't be able to harm you. Similarly, saying *"I am Brahma"* will transform you into *Brahma* until even birth and death cannot affect you. Try to understand everything from this point of view. If you get into the habit of thinking in this way it will become a part of you.

You people do not have a firm belief in anyone or anything. You move from place to place, and from Guru to Guru. You do not gain anything from this entertainment of going to so many Gurus and assimilating everyone's point of view. By trying to learn too much from too many you remain a zero and stay where you are. I do not tell you to do any penance or hard spiritual practice (*sadhana*). At the most I may tell you to chant the name of God (*Brahma japa*). Keep the vital breath busy with this chanting. Allot this work of repeating the name of God to your vital breath and then just stand back and watch. Just as you allot work to your cook and then watch him cooking, keep the vital breath continuously busy with the recitation. You will then begin to hear this recitation throughout your body.

You should have an intense desire to seek the Truth. Only then will the results be quick. The outcome of *japa* will be according to the strength of your conviction and the extent of your faith. My Guru did a lot of penance and long spiritual practice before he got this knowledge. But without my having had to do any penance or spiritual practice, he bestowed this knowledge upon me. I am not dependent upon this world or this universe; this world and this universe depend upon Me. How do you recognize me? What identity do you allot to me and how do you judge me? With what identity do you judge yourselves? You entertain the idea that you are going to have different births. I don't believe in any such stories. I know 'I' never was. That "I Amness" was never there for me. I am the unborn state.

V: I am listening very closely. Will this intensity deepen my understanding?

M: You are already spontaneous, so why talk about what doesn't exist at all? It is all an illusion. Whenever great scholars or sages visit me, I don't prepare myself for the discussion with them. I say whatever comes to me. Ultimately, I know that even these words are like the children of a barren woman!

V: Do we show our ignorance by asking questions to liven the discussion?

M: What is knowledge? Knowledge takes birth only in ignorance and ignorance is the parent of knowledge.

Everything is
conceptual

Visitor: What is the meaning of "I Am," the basic illusion?

Maharaj: It means 'pure', even though you have to provide food for it. A *yogi* had been studying the art of reviving objects after death. One day he saw a bone in the forest and decided to practice his art to see how effective it was. He chanted a *mantra* and suddenly a lion appeared. He did not, however, create any food for the lion and so when the lion was hungry he ate the *yogi*. The moral of this story is that before you create anything, you have to first create food. The "I Am" is sustained by the food-body. That is our body, which is the food for the "I Am." Every creature depends upon its food and the "I Am" depends upon our body. Will you remember this?

When you recite the *mantra* relating to a particular god, that particular quality in Consciousness is created within you. *Rama, Krishna, Brahma, Shiva* are only the incarnations of your Consciousness. The same Consciousness that 'You are' is also what these gods, which have been created with various names from your Consciousness, 'are'.

V: There is a statue of Nityananda in his ashram. Muktananda says that Nityananda is still alive and that he communicates with him. What do you say about that?

M: I also have many photographs of my Guru here. Because my Guru 'is' I know "I Am." You presume that your Guru Nityananda is a body-mind and that is the mistake. I do not look upon my Guru like that. He is merged into Consciousness and I see him as That. So long as the body is there, Consciousness and memory are there. Once the body is gone, the Consciousness is unaware of anything. When the oil is there, the flame keeps burning by using the oil, but no oil is used after the flame is gone. Whatever is burnt is burnt and whatever remains, remains. When the child is born, growth takes place. The "I Am" is there throughout his or her life even if a person lives for 100 years, but the "I Am" disappears when the body is gone. This is called death.

I would like to know your opinion about what I have told you. Should I tell you all of this or should I keep quiet? Somebody came this morning who kept quoting his Guru, so I sent him back to his Guru. By listening to me seriously, people could lose all hope and ambition. Because they want to take action in the world, hope should be there for them. If they feel that they are not gaining anything here, they should go away. Why should I talk to these people who want to live and achieve something? Nityananda hardly ever talked, but his disciple Muktananda goes on talking and has created an empire. Chinmayananda has done the same thing although now he says he wants to stop talking and go away to the Himalayas. All my expounding will only lead people to a state of inaction, so why should I talk? Anyway, whatever you have heard here can never be erased and will have its effect.

V: I want to develop my determination to be in the "I Am."

M: Did you have any Consciousness when you did not have your body? You may have as much faith as you want, but even that will be gone when the body is no more, as your Consciousness will not be there. Where are you without your Consciousness? There is nothing for you to do. Everything just comes into being and happens. Why are you concerned with what to do? You deal with the world only after having Consciousness, when the "I Am" is there. Once it is gone, everything ends. It is all spontaneous.

Every nation has had different rulers ruling the country at different times, who are now dead and gone. Do they come back and ask how the country is being ruled now? Does Christ come back and ask why you go to India to listen to all of this trash? By presuming to be on one side, you take up cudgels against different faiths and spill blood in the name of religion. Our Hindu deities are supposed to be very powerful, but did they do anything when Muslim and Christian invaders came to rule over India? We all had parents. Where are they once they have died? You just say they have gone home to God, but are they here now? Do they come and interfere in our daily lives? We go on looking for a Guru to guide us. What did Ramakrishna say to Vivekananda? He just said, *"Take the ripe mango and enjoy it. Don't keep questioning where the mango has come from, etc."*

The worry about death does not affect me at all. Why are you worried about reincarnation? Just experience whatever is happening to you now. I was asked why I previously told some people that many births are needed before realization can happen. I have to tell such stories to ignorant people. When a person describes a memory of his last birth, I ask him whether he remembers who his parents were, animals or human beings? You are only talking about your dream. At present you can say who your parents are, but do you know who they were during your last birth? If you cannot remember anything, then just say it is all over and finished. It is just a dream; forget about it.

What others say about how rebirth is determined by the thoughts you have when you are dying is mere hearsay. What I am telling you about the merging of the "I Am" with the Source is the real thing. This world has existed for millions of years. Male and Female, *Purusha* and *Prakriti*, have created so many dynasties. From which background have you come to this present form? Did you come from your father's father or your mother's mother? From the time of the first couple ever created, which birth is this? Can you go back and find out? Why carry that tension around with you when you cannot really know or remember any of it? Don't bother about it.

As you progress and get established in Beingness, you will understand that you are above the dreaming and waking states, as these only pertain to your "I Amness." We are only able to observe because of this "I Amness." When the "I Amness" is not there, the tool required to observe is also not there. Once there is Self-realization, the whole riddle is solved. What *Krishna* preaches in the Gita is correct. What I am saying is of no profit or loss. Even a blind person can describe a huge well; how does he know? It is just a way of expressing his thoughts.

As life flows, go on doing what has to be done. However much you run around, without God's Will there is nothing. Whether it is your dreams or your visions, whatever you see is nothing but God's appearance. It is the Source, or Consciousness, which is appearing in so many forms. Everything is conceptual.

Identify with the body,
suffer with the body

Maharaj: While the knowledge is getting established, you will be in a sleep-like state – even witnessing won't be there. You will feel as if you are asleep, but it is not sleep. It is called *Udmani*, which means 'above the level of the mind'. The *yogis* and sages are in that state above the mind. It is a state that transcends the mind. When I talk, I am talking from the *Udmani* state – from Nothingness. It is a restful and relaxed state.

Visitor: Is it a state of deep sleep?

M: Although it feels similar to sleep, it is not sleep, because there is Awareness or Consciousness deep inside. You will not have this experience unless you are stabilized in peace and stillness.

V: When I am reading, sometimes there is an identity, and I see myself reading. Is that different from the state you compared it with?

M: While dreaming, you observe the dream don't you? At that time, the whole dream world is in front of you. You simultaneously watch what is happening while also taking part in the dream world as one of the characters, one of the actors. But here, you are purely a Witness. You are not acting but are merely a Witness, whereas there you also participate in the dream.

Some Gurus give disciplines which only engage the mental aspect and activity. They get their disciples involved in the play of the mind by referring to the concepts that appeal to them. They concretize their preferred concepts in the form of activities for their disciples. Leave all that alone – there is no question of effort and no question of elevating oneself to a higher level. Where will this spark or flame go? Where will my vital breath or *prana* go? There is no question of it going anywhere. You only have to be aware as the Witness and you will merge with the five elements.

If you identify with the body-mind, you will have to undergo all of its suffering and misery, while facing its effects. If you identify with the body you will suffer with the body. A swimmer, when caught in a whirlpool, has to go down deep beneath the whirlpool, then swim beyond its diameter before coming up to the surface. If the swimmer struggles, he will become exhausted and will be finished. Similarly, with this whirlpool of the body-mind, before you become panicky dive down underneath – do not get entangled with the body-mind. Go deep beyond the thoughts and come into the thoughtless state. I tell you to ask me questions because I want to find out the depth of your understanding. The questions are of the mind, but *You* are not the mind.

First there was the desire to 'Be'. From this "I Am," the air came first and the earth last. Then from the earth came the vegetation and the many forms of life, each having this "I Amness." Because of the five elements you have the body, and in that body is the "I Amness." What you call death is when the vital breath goes back into the air and the body merges into the five elements. When the vital breath separates from the body, the "I Amness" disappears.

If you come to me as a man you may get something for your livelihood, but that will be your only gift. However, if you come to me understanding that you are God, that knowledge will manifest. For example, if there is a vacancy in an office offering a salary of 10,000 rupees a month, only a suitable man will get the job as an unqualified man would not be able to last. Similarly, only people who consider themselves as *Brahman* can get that knowledge. Other people, who identify with the body-consciousness, are not fit for it.

You must have maturity and you must be worthy of the knowledge that you want to gain. By chanting "*I am Brahman*" you become subtle and escape this sense of body-mind. If you go to other so-called Gurus, they will tell you something relating to your body-mind sense, and tell you that if you follow certain disciplines they might grant you something. But you will not be able to attain that *Brahma*-hood. You must first accept that you are without a body-mind and that you are subtle. That sense must be instilled in you.

I look to this *Brahma* state, my Beingness ("I Amness"), and observe my body – like an incense stick with a spark on it. That chemical, or seer, is here in this incense stick, and is being burned by that spark. You must become initiated into the understanding of what I am expounding to you. I am telling you about the seed of *Brahman*. You have to understand that I am planting the *Brahma* seed in you. That *Brahma* seed is your Beingness ("I Amness"), which sprouts into manifestation. That *Brahma* state does not require anything to eat. It has no hunger, because *Brahma* alone embraces everything and all manifestation is *Brahma*. I am trying to raise you to that state. Do not think you can become a realized soul only by listening to a few lectures here. You have to forget everything and merge with *Brahman*.

V: What is the difference between worldly knowledge and knowledge about Brahman?

M: You will not realize it unless the difference within you goes. If you think you are the body you cannot gain this knowledge. Who wants to know about *Brahman*? Find that out first, and then change the identity of that I from body-consciousness to 'I am one with *Brahman*'. Focus on that *Brahman* instead of on the body-mind. You must understand yourself correctly. You think that I am a man, and being a man means being conditioned by body and mind. How can you understand the *Brahma* state from this standpoint?

V: Does this mean that Brahma knowledge merely comes from the fact that "I Am?"

M: Who is it that needs to understand this the most, the knowledge that "I Am?" If you listen carefully and imbibe the principles, you will get rid of this body-mind sense and dwell only in the "I Amness" (Beingness). I am the love of Beingness, and Beingness itself is love.

V: The "I Amness" precludes the aspect of "I am not," doesn't it?

M: You want to know the link, the bridge, between "I Am" and "I am not," is that it? First of all only hold on to the "I Amness," without any words, and just 'Be'. When somebody hails you, you respond, but before you do so there is somebody within you who becomes aware of the call and the need to answer. That being is the "I Am," and he has been there even before that awareness appeared.

V: Does the flash of light come from Beingness – "I Am?"

M: The moment the "I Amness" explodes or appears, all of space is lit up. The entire sky is the expression of your Beingness. Even though this whole world is an expression of your Beingness, you believe that you are only the body. Your love for the body limits your horizons. But the moment those walls come down, you are one with *Brahman* and the whole universe.

The illusion appears true because of attachment to the body

Visitor: Maharaj, I have the feeling that I was 'killed' by you last night.

Maharaj: If you know this, then where else will you go to look for different holy men (*sadhus*) and further knowledge? Maybe you will feel very proud after getting this knowledge and grow a beard, put on some garlands and beads, and sit with a posture! Rajneesh has understood this principle. Because he knows that there is nothing in any of this, he makes a big show and makes people dance around him. Where have you come from?

V: We have come from France. What is the tangible principle that you have, and can your mind point out the vital breath?

M: Can you hold the vital breath with your mind?

V: How can I transform the intellectual understanding into inside awareness?

M: Can you describe your colour or your body form? Be one with the knowledge, you are already complete. What is it that you want to assimilate?

V: *Maybe there is nothing to assimilate. Maybe when one gets established in the "I Am" it is all clear.*

M: When you mix sugar with water you can say that you have some sweet water. But is there any difference when you mix water with water? Only water can be completely one with water.

V: *When you describe Purusha as the male force and Prakriti as the female force, it seems you are giving it some shape and form.*

M: What is the difference between nature and man? Can you differentiate between man and woman without referring to the body form?

V: *How can I?*

M: Show me the difference between the name of a god and my name?

V: *There is no difference.*

M: Yet you are still convinced that you are going to die.

V: *I am not too convinced about that anymore.*

M: Is her reply acceptable to all of you?

Another V: No.

M: Are you stupid? She only came here yesterday, but you have been coming here for the past two years. In what way do you disagree with her reply?

V: I cannot say I agree or disagree, because it is her experience.

M: You are still not worthy of this knowledge. You have listened to me for two years and yet today I still had to convince you that there is no body. What you think is the body is only the food-body. After the body dies, if nothing is done about it, the worms will eat it. The body is the food – that is the body. The body will die, but you are not the body so you are not going to die. So, where is the doubt? You don't have any birth, so you don't have any death. If the lady who has attended these talks for two days is convinced, while you remain unconvinced after two years, what have you learned? I am beyond death. When you awake within the dream, *maya* and nature no longer exist. The illusion appears true because of attachment to the body, but once the vital breath leaves the body, the body ceases to exist and the identity is gone.

V: Last night, I awoke from my sleep feeling that everything is nonsense and it is all an illusion.

M: This whole thing is based on illusion. How can it be real? It is this unreality that looks real because of the body form. Once this body is gone and cremated, the illusion will be gone. That reality which you pick out from the unreal cannot be lasting, because its very foundation is unreal.

V: *This entire universe is my Self?*

M: All this is your Self. But, when will you eat? As long as you are bound by a body that feels hunger, you cannot be one with the universe.

V: *What difference does this make?*

M: How old are you?

V: *Forty-six years old.*

M: Give me some piece of information about yourself, two days prior to your forty-six years. If you cannot remember that, how can you swallow all of this knowledge? Your Consciousness cannot swallow this big tree, which grew from a small seed. There is no space required for the dream world. It has its existence solely in the knowledge of Beingness. Similarly, all of this illusion and knowledge has existence only through our being conscious of it. Your birthday and birth time – is it not the creation of your mind? How long do you intend to stay here to get established in the knowledge?

V: *As long as it feels relevant.*

M: In that case, is the knowledge real or is it a cheat?

V: *A cheat with a smile.*

M: If you tap on the cheek of a small baby, it will smile at you and you will smile back. The smile of the child and your emanation are the same. So, is the smile of the child going to die? The quality of Beingness, like the smile of the child, comes and goes. The one who understands this is beyond birth and death.

In the Hindu tradition it is said that in your old age you must become a renunciate (*sannyasi*). Two months ago, the Italian ambassador came here with four elderly gentlemen who had the intention of becoming renunciates. After listening to this talk, they gave up their idea of renunciation. Normally, the renunciation (*sannyas*) is concerned with six aspects: the five elements and the knowledge "I Am." But when you understand all of this, what is the point in renouncing these six qualities? When all of this knowledge is imbibed by you and settled in you, there will be no more desires and you will not be attached. You will be beyond desire and no-desire, and you will be unconcerned.

As an example, seeing you walking on the road, a taxi driver offers to take you to your destination. He takes you round and round and finally brings you home, charging you an exorbitant fare. You come out of the house in the evening and realize that you had picked the taxi up very near to where you wanted to go in the first place. The taxi driver brought you home in a very round about way. Other guides or Gurus like Rajneesh are like this. They show you a long and difficult path to achieve *Brahman*, or Self-realization. Although we are attached to the whole world and are moving about in it, the root of our attachment is Self-love – knowledge of one's existence.

V: I like your teaching, as it is the Truth. So where is Rajneesh's moral sense and responsibility as a teacher?

M: It is all fun. He knows it is not real, and he wants to have all the fun. That is his idea and his concept. And he also wants to create a peace clan.

V: If he is enlightened how can he create that illusion?

M: It is all fun. All of the disciples are ignorant, so he has fun with them, or makes fun of them. I did a lot of *japa* and a lot of penance but I got nothing. I eventually found the right Guru and in a moment I was transformed. When I met that great Guru (*Sadguru**) – unfragmented, whole, unblemished, and complete – I became That. Have self-confidence or faith. If this knowledge is totally absorbed by you, you will not need any words or sacred recitation to achieve the Ultimate.

---

* Sadguru – this may refer to Maharaj's own Guru or to Consciousness, God Himself, who is the Guru of Gurus.

Whatever is created is by the knowledge "I Am"

Maharaj: Waking up happens to the body.

Visitor: Something was aware of this body.

M: The Witness cannot 'Be' in the absence of the knowledge "I Am." Who are you seeing if you are not aware of the "I Am?" You have covered everything with this "I Am" knowledge. The five elemental world is only the creation of this "I Amness."

V: Is there any knowledge of the state of transition from the Absolute to the "I Am?"

M: Don't ponder on that transition stage for the time being. Dwell instead on the fact that your own Consciousness is the whole universe, and 'Be' there. Be cautious when such experiences arise that you get That experience – be alert here to the "I Am" and all other experiences will be transcended.

The next elevation will only come when you abide in the Self. When you are convinced that "all of Consciousness is my Self," when this conviction is firmly embedded, then only will the question of the next elevation arise. Dwell on the principle of that state for a sufficiently long time. All the greatness, significance, and magnificence of the entire world is dwelling in the principle 'You are' and "I Am." That is the prop and that itself is the greatness. There is no other remedy, no other path, except implicit faith and conviction in the Self. There is no alternative.

You are still fidgety.

V: *The body does whatever it wants.*

M: You have all this excitement because you feel happy with the knowledge that you have received. Whatever knowledge you have heard and accepted intellectually, you have to 'Be'. Take it that you are That. 'That' means no shape and no design. Whatever you see pertains only to That, to your "I Amness." Spontaneously 'It is'! *You* are that principle. Don't try to unravel this with your intellect. Just observe and accept it as it is.

V: *When do you get these experiences, etc.?*

M: Whatever is created is created by the knowledge "I Am." Do not pursue this path of running after experiences. Your own Consciousness creates everything.

V: Will there not be extreme loneliness from that experience of "I Amness?"

M: Be patient, don't be presumptuous. You are asking a very deep question. You have to listen first, then contemplate and meditate. Only then can you ask such questions.

V: I have experienced that complete loneliness. Seeing everything as 'me' makes one feel very lonely.

M: Why do you always fragment the Witness? Everything is *You*.

V: And that is the experience of complete loneliness.

M: You have still not recognized that little remnant. First of all, are you fully convinced that you are not an individual?

V: No.

M: Then don't ask the question. Only when you are convinced that you are not a conditioned man, conditioned by body and mind, may you ask such questions. What is God? All greatness is because of the "I Am." There is no other path, only this conviction. This is it! The name and body arise from the "I Am." When hungry, if you want to know 'who' is hungry, just observe. You think that you have understood everything, but it is not so. *You* are the one who is listening to all of this. 'Who' has understood this? *You* are all that has ever been created. Only *You* are there.

V: This knowledge is a new seed and it is just taking root.

M: Who is the seed? This knowledge is ancient (*sanatan*). It has come from Eternity. From the eternal Absolute, which is ever there, a seed appears; that seed is the "I Amness." It appears spontaneously; its remnant is in us. This little seed sprouts and the whole world is created. If the morning talks have affected you, then any bodily disciplines will be redundant. They are superfluous and will have no effect on you. Do you remember the state that I was addressing in the morning talk? Both states are identical. Fully imbibe what I spoke to you about in the morning and become one with That. If you do not like this or cannot accept it, forget everything and do what you like.

V: I will not leave you, Maharaj.

M: In the case of a devotee (*bhakta*), initially the devotee does not want to leave God. Later on, even if the devotee asks God to go, God will not leave him. God means the knowledge "I Am." The knowledge "I Am" is God (*Bhagavan*). I have been talking for more than eighty years, but this knowledge still doesn't leave me. Is it not enough? What have you to say on this particular point? Although I am trying to throw the principle overboard it won't leave me, and even if I wanted to, I cannot cling to it.

V: What is the principle you can't throw away or cling to?

M: Since everything is *You*, you can't cut it away from you. This knowledge of "I Amness" is part of you. How can you throw it away? And where can you throw it? When you are established in Beingness ("I Amness"), you realize that everything is *You*. It is all *Your* creation.

A state of no-mind
with you as Nothingness

Visitor: What happens to the body form?

Maharaj: Will it become like dry earth in due course? No, it is not like that. When the water falls the grass will grow again on that dry earth.

V: Maharaj, I always want to be with you from now on.

M: Since you have understood me, are you going to marry me?

V: Yes.

M: Understand the significance of what I am saying. I do not own a body-mind. I have transcended the body-mind and have no identification with it. Neither of us have a body or mind, so who will marry whom? It is all One. I am already wedded, but without any separate identity of name and form.

That principle, "I Am," is your illusion, but the Oneness got rid of that illusion. Then, one is without body or mind. The principle of Oneness has no shape, therefore male and female also have no shape – this is the wedding of male and female. At that stage the barren woman conceives and progeny is delivered! That is the "I Am" state and that is the universe. But that Oneness is not a state of illusion. Does anyone want to oppose and challenge this?

V: Can you explain the higher state of bliss and is it the same as "I Amness?"

M: Bliss (*Satchidananda*) is a superior quality of happiness. However, it is a bliss that is not permanent; it's still just a state of mind. Realization is when this state of mind, this bliss, dissolves or disappears into a neutral state without quality or form (*nirguna*). This is realization. This is a state of no-mind or no thought, where you permanently remain a zero, a Nothingness.

What is your age?

V: Thirty-eight years old.

M: What was your idea of bliss two years prior to your birth?

V: I would not know about that.

M: At that time, two years prior to your birth, you had no

experience of the dreaming or waking states, or of pleasure and pain. That means that you had absolutely no experience whatsoever. Do you agree?

V: *Experience needs a body.*

M: Only give a reply to what I ask you, say yes or no.

V: *No.*

M: Does it mean that *You* were not? Who says, "I did not have any experience?" Please come forward.

V: *Thank you for pushing me inside myself.*

M: If you were inside you would not be able to get back out again. Who is being pushed inside? Think about it and then answer. When *You* were not, where is the question of bringing you back or forward? Bliss only came into existence once there was the union of male and female. Otherwise there was no bliss. You are the product of that bliss. You are thirty-eight years from that bliss, but it is only now that you know it. At that time you did not know. Till the age of three you never knew what that bliss was. Thereafter you may have had glimpses of it, but only now do you know. All of these are the remembrances or the remnants of that bliss.

V: *Do we carry that memory of Oneness like when we were in the womb?*

M: How do you know that? When you were in your mother's womb, it was only a chemical that was working. You were born when that chemical completed its work. Was this ever explained to you when you were at Rajneesh's ashram? Were the teachings there for the students to enjoy that bliss? Have you been there? Tell the truth.

V: I just experienced a lot of suffering.

M: That was not the question. Do not stray from the question. Were you aware that he was enjoying things in that way – not him personally, but was he encouraging the bliss-seeking there?

V: No, I don't think he did that.

M: I do not agree. The people there were dancing and embracing each other, and jumping and rolling on the floor. Isn't that correct?

V: Yes, that was in my ignorance when I took phenomena for reality, but now I will not go there.

M: At that time, did you call those movements joy or *Satchidananda*? Who was it that was dancing in those moments? Can you say? I want an answer from you.

V: I am still in the process.

M: You may be in any process but I want an answer *(laughter)*. How did they get this bliss? In the process of becoming parents they derived the pleasure of *Satchidananda*. Are you listening?

V: Yes.

M: Will you be wandering elsewhere now searching for spiritual teachers?

V: No, as soon as I saw you, Maharaj, it was all over.

M: The one who is searching after spiritual matters, is he alive or dead? In the process of understanding, the Self — the knowledge, the Consciousness — became birth-less and death-less. *(Maharaj sips some water.)* No water, no talk — all is well. It is because that body feeling is encompassed in your veins. When that goes away everything will be one body. I am only talking in reference to the body; inside and outside only pertain to the body. The One inside has no birth or death.

The knowledge that 'You are' creates your world

Maharaj: Do you remember what we discussed in the morning?

Visitor: Yes, you are bringing me to that point of awareness.

M: Even this idea, or having this concept, is not correct. Just as the sweetness of sugar is right there in each grain, this knowledge of "I Amness" that is there in you contains the whole universe. I am not expounding this knowledge for the benefit of a human being, the one who is involved with the body-mind; it is being expounded to that state of Divinity within you.

V: Is there communication on two levels?

M: When you first came here you were involved with the body-mind and the talk then was on that level. Now it is being expounded in relation to your Beingness, the

"I Amness," which having created the universe is dwelling within you as the remnant. The very core of that knowledge 'You are' contains the whole universe. As an example, in the dream world the knowledge 'You are' has to be there before the dream world is created. Similarly, the knowledge 'You are' must be there for this world of yours. The knowledge that 'You are' creates your world.

V: I don't understand the translation. It is like there is music going on in the room and I am deaf and cannot hear the music.

M: The one who is deaf should not listen to the music (laughter). You are like a person who goes on searching for himself in every nook and corner of the room. You are looking for something that is already within you. You cannot find the Ultimate Truth by looking outside.

V: It is like you are banging on my head to help me remember.

M: This idea of yours is also not correct. Get out of your body sense. Your body is made out of the five elements, but is not You. This body that you think is your whole world, is not permanent. As long as you are identified with the body you are a sick person and still not ready for realization. When you totally realize that 'You are', but not conditioned by this body-mind, you will be one with the whole world. This universe is created by that knowledge alone.

V: I am not able to swallow the medicine you are trying to give me.

M: You will need to do meditation and recitation of sacred words or *mantras* so that this obstacle of your body-sense will be eliminated.

V: Will you give me a mantra?

M: Actually it is not necessary. Just watch the Self and hear that sound that is already going on within. It appears that you have no time to be still and steady. Presently you are very attached to the sensations of the outside world that you get through the body-mind state. Ignore outside attractions and go within. You will then find your real Self. You seem to have forgotten what you heard here in the morning and are now raising new points.

V: Why should I stick to memories?

M: Who is sticking to memories? The knowledge that 'You are' is subtler than the sky, so how can memory stick to it? Let it be.

V: Earlier you were talking about 'accidents' and life-spans. Were you talking in reference to the Bhagavad Gita?

M: It was with reference to life and death, not to the Gita. When I talk I refer to the "I Am" knowledge, and not to me personally. As long as you are attached to and identified with the body you will never have peace. But once you get rid of the body-attachment you could be the king and ruler of the world, yet still be at peace. Suppose whilst talking I uttered a bad word to all of you. You would go home and say, *"I went to Maharaj's place and he insulted me."* Is that not so? But if I tell you that this divine knowledge that 'You are' is the creator of your universe and, after creating, its remnant is embedded within you, you do not remember or understand what I have told you. Am I correct?

V: Yes and no.

M: Why are you saying 'yes and no'? That means you have no faith in me. If you have no faith you can leave.

The spark
of "I Amness"

Maharaj: Out of the body of the incense stick, according to the colour and fragrance, everything flows. Its destiny is sealed in that. Similarly, our destiny is also sealed in the causal body which is formed out of the essences that are consumed. Out of the food-essence body, worms, insects, etc. and human beings are formed. The lower species have their own way of communication with each other and it is called *Vachaspati*. Human beings alone have the quality of intelligence and are called *Brihaspati*, which means 'master of intellect'. *Shukra* means 'seed or essence of life'. The father provides the quality of Beingness that is in the seed form, and the blood of the mother provides the energy. Once it is formed into shape, the seed loses its existence. Without food or nourishment there cannot be any life. The knowledge of Beingness is everything. Wandering here and there will not bring you peace. Hopes and desires will always be there, but once you understand and absorb what I am saying you will cease to be there. Then, who will have these desires and who will be there to enjoy them?

Visitor: The will to live is strong. To drop this identification with the body is like dying in a sense. Is it possible to do it voluntarily?

M: What you call the body is this food, which is the fuel for the sustenance of your Consciousness. The mind is the product of the vital breath; when the vital breath flows the mind flows and creates the world. Language is an external impression that's made on the child. The child absorbs the vital breath and then talks. Consciousness is the wish to 'Be'. That Beingness wants to be perpetuated and does not want to be extinguished. Its quality is the will to live, which is love itself. It loves to live. Because it wants to live and sustain itself, it creates the right conditions and goes into activity in the world.

V: Isn't this detachment from the body-mind like a form of death?

M: Yes, it is a sort of death. (*Maharaj sings a morning prayer.*) "*The greatest advantage I've got is out of the fact that I am enjoying this living death.*" Most of the saints talk about this living death.

V: Can we reach a state like you, where we are willing to experience this death?

M: You don't lose your Self. The whole process is to understand your mis-identification and come out of it. If you accept this then nothing can touch you. Knowing that you are not the body, watch the vital breath as a flow of the mind. You are here in the spark of "I Amness." When you acknowledge the "I Amness" you become the spark. I am like space and do not have an identity – this is my "I Amness" from which all the talk is being produced.

Now you have heard me talk at length. Do you still feel it necessary to have all this play of dancing and jumping about in Rajneesh's ashram to achieve Self-realization?

V: No.

M: A common man who feels inclined towards spirituality will be full of concepts. Unless he is made to dance and jump about he will not understand the futility of the mind and its concepts. Only then will he come here to listen to these talks. Chinmayananda is another Guru who talks about the Upanishads. When his disciples find that they cannot relate to the Upanishads they come here to learn about Self-realization. Muktananda's followers have also come and have never gone back.

V: I went through all this nonsense for ten years. It was necessary, only because it gave me discrimination, to be able to recognize the diamond teachings of Maharaj.

M: There is no God. There is no devotion. I am neither a saint nor a Guru. I am not learned, nor do I have any pride of knowledge. Is that acceptable to you?

Interpreter to M: It is acceptable because I have heard you talk for a long time, but if I had heard you say it on my first visit I would not have come again.

V: I would not have had the maturity ten years ago to understand you, Maharaj.

M: Now that you have heard me, tell me what is your identity, name, and form?

V: I have only one obsession – to get rid of all ideas of form and shape.

M: It is already not there (*laughter*); it is absolutely not.

V: I will have to go deeper and find out.

M: Who is going to find out? Where is the person who is going to search? You had a burden of ten sticks, but all of the sticks have been thrown out. So where is the burden? The essence of the five elements is within you, but are *You* the five elements? The sweet made with *ghee* is very nourishing, but I am not that. If you throw away this flower in my hand, will I be thrown away along with it? I eat food, but am I that food? Whatever food is not needed is thrown out, but does that mean I am also thrown out?

The key that
switches on the *lila*

Visitor: The dialogue going on inside me is constantly interrupting whatever I am hearing from you. What can I do?

Maharaj: Our friend who was sitting near the window changed his seat earlier because of the loud music and noise from the outside that distracted him from listening to my talk. In this new seat, the noise outside ceased to disturb him. Similarly, we should move our attention away from the chatter within, observing it only as a witness, unconcerned about it. Then the chatter will not disturb us. If we try to resist it, it will disturb us even more. Do not try to judge whether it is good or bad. When I am paying attention to you and you are listening attentively to me, the noise coming through the window will not disturb either of us. At present the noise outside has stopped by itself. Similarly, that chattering within you will also settle by itself.

V: Is becoming established in the Beingness like maya saying 'I am leaving' and Brahma saying 'I am staying'?

M: Just 'Be'. The sunlight will go when the sun sets. So when the *maya* goes the Beingness or Consciousness will settle. Your attention should be focused on the Beingness. Don't worry about *maya* or anything else. In that state, *maya* will serve you with folded hands. Anandamayi is established and one with her Beingness. As a result, *maya* is serving her with a lot of affluence and everybody goes and falls at her feet.

Is this your first visit to Mumbai? From where have you come?

V: I have travelled alone from France.

M: Who told you to come here?

V: I read the book 'I Am That'. Maybe it will take months for me to understand all of it.

M: Yes, stabilizing in it will take time. The knowledge within you has to mature and slowly get established.

V: Is it necessary to suffer because of what is happening around us?

M: It is only the mind. You should not allow it to get affected by all that you see. If the talks had any effect on you, you would not have asked any questions referring to body-consciousness or your experiences. When you remember constantly that you are not the body, the effect will lessen.

V: I am sorry I have been so stupid.

M: The ideas which you have expressed only relate to stupidity. Yesterday I gave you the example of *Paruna* (male) and *Paruni* (female). *Paruna* means 'youth'. If you split this Marathi word in two, '*paru*' and '*anu*', you get 'tree' and 'atom'. Atom refers to the seed. This tree exists because of that seed or atom which is your Consciousness. All of this has arisen because of Consciousness. Now what will the next action be? This tree will again unite its male (*Paruna*) and female (*Paruni*) parts to create more seeds, in order for more universes to grow. So what is the power of youth? It reproduces in the same image.

I told you yesterday that this body is the food for other species, or for itself, or for the sustenance of its own Consciousness. Once you know that you are not in this world permanently, you will have no need to hoard material possessions. Does the name that you are referred to by have any shape or colour? If this is the edible matter for your knowledge, are you this body? I eat bread, but I am not the bread that sustains and nourishes my body. Are you the breath? Are you the quality of "I Amness" that is there because of the food-body? When the food-body is dropped, the breath is also dropped. How can that "I Amness" be sustained then? The "I Amness" will also disappear.

V: What is the progress after "I Amness?"

M: Unless you have the understanding of "I Amness" there is no progress. Once you understand the "I Am" there is nothing further to understand. When your "I Amness" is gone, together with everything, then there is nothing. Then that Nothingness is everything. Who is saying this?

V: Is it the "I Amness" that is saying that there is nothing and that nothing is everything?

M: Once you know the "I Am" there is no one left to say that nothing is everything.

(*A woman who thinks she is a Guru, and a disciple of hers who are among the visitors, now enter into a dialogue with Maharaj.*)

Visiting Guru: When the "I Am" goes into Nothingness, it is the Nothingness that says there is nothing.

M: Your Nothingness is telling whom? Is it a fact that she claims to be your Guru?

Disciple: Do you know who my Guru is?

M: If I know your Guru, what is the use of that to you? Only if you know your Guru can he or she be of any use to you.

Visiting Guru: The step from the ego to the Total Consciousness is the step that I am missing.

M: Who says that she has missed this step?

Disciple: Small ego to Total Consciousness. The lady who asked the question forgets this step.

M: Who are you to say that she forgets? If you say she is your Guru, how dare you say that she is making a mistake?

Disciple: We are one. I am merging with my Guru.

M: I asked you whether you have understood the key that switches on the play (*lila*). I want a reply.

Visiting Guru: No, I don't understand the key.

M: What is your age?

Visiting Guru: I am ageless.

M: What is the age of your body?

Visiting Guru: This body is about sixty years of age.

M: Did you hear or see the *lila* when the body was not there?

Visiting Guru: I was the lila.

M: You are telling a lie. At that time you did not have any concept of the knowledge "I Am" – the Beingness.

Visiting Guru: So does that make me a liar?

M: Since you are a Guru you are trying to run away with it. You only had an experience of this '*lila*' after you acquired this body. Answer me, yes or no?

Visiting Guru: I had the memory of this experience in another body as well.

M: What is the food that sustains your memory? The body is your food, is it not? Your body is the sustenance of this experience of '*lila*', and your "I Amness" only appeared when this body of yours came into existence.

Visiting Guru: The memory is in the brain and it is like a computer, which is part of my mind.

M: The brain is created only when the body is created. When you did not have this body did you have the memory? Don't give explanations. Just answer, yes or no?

Visiting Guru: I don't know.

M: Did you have any memory before the existence of this body? When the body was not there you did not know 'You were'. Answer me, yes or no?

Visiting Guru: All right. Yes.

Identify yourself
with Consciousness

Maharaj: What was the cause for the formation of your body which allowed you to understand that 'You are'? This body is born because of the action of the parents. Is it not so?

Visitor: I see it as energy.

M: You may call it whatever you like. Is it not because of the action of the parents that your body, which sustains your Consciousness, was formed?

V: Certainly.

M: After the body comes into existence, whatever happens is an illusion or play. What is the use of all this to you?

V: It is useless and senseless to me.

M: If you think that all this *lila* is senseless and you've come to the conclusion that all is unreal, what advantage can you derive from it? The saints call this renunciation and are not interested in it. Once you understand all this, your body, the knowledge, and everything else is useless. What other knowledge do you want or seek?

V: All I want is to be purified and good.

M: Whatever name has been given to you, can you make it clean by polishing it? So why did you say that you want to be pure and good?

V: I want to be without all this.

M: If you want to be without all this, then in what shape or image would you like to be? When I am talking to this lady, I want to know whether all of you are listening or not. Do you understand what I am saying?

Visiting Guru: Yes, we understand.

M: Does it mean that you and the world have been thrown overboard?

Visiting Guru: I am not committing myself to anything.

M: Who does not want to commit to anything? How can you be caught? Why are you showing off? This girl who is fighting thinks she is a Guru! What have you to say, Guru of Ramandas? (*The girl starts singing.*) There is no need for this song.

All this is illusion. What I am saying is itself illusion. This entire congregation here is only the effect of *maya*.

Visiting Guru: You, Maharaj, are also illusion.

M: I am watching the *maya*. The incense stick, the spark, the fragrance that is inhaled, is all illusion and I am watching it all. I do not deliberately do anything; I just witness all of it. Do not get attached. Have you understood all that I have told you? Why does your breath not run away with the breeze of this electric fan?

Visiting Guru: I have come here to know about God and not about the electric fan.

M: This God is just a word. What is the difference between this name God and your name?

Visiting Guru: None.

M: Then what enquiry are you making about God?

Visiting Guru: I am not.

Interpreter: You said earlier, "I have come here to know about God."

M: You have an idea that you are a Guru and are clinging from that standpoint to various concepts and ideas. I am a free man and am not attached to anything. The talk just happens.

Visiting Guru: You are laughing at me and trapping me in my mind.

M: So long as you are proud and think that you are a Guru, or anything else, you will not have any peace. She says that she has come to study *Ayurveda*, yet she thinks she is a Guru.

Visiting Guru: You are absolutely right.

M: You have asked some interesting questions. Are you going to visit again?

Visiting Guru: Yes, because you are so adorable and cute.

Interpreter to V: The word adorable is translated in Marathi as 'pujya', which also means zero. So, do you mean Maharaj is a zero?

Visiting Guru: Yes.

M: Buddha described the final state as *shunyata* or zero – void. Are you studying *Ayurveda*? Do you know what *Ayurveda* means?

Visiting Guru: It is a Veda.

M: '*Ayur*' means the life-span. In *Ayurvedic* medicine they conserve the life energy to prolong life. An *Ayurvedic* doctor gives medicine to the patient and saves his life; say yes or no? If the patient wants to live then the answer is 'yes', otherwise the answer is 'no'.

Visiting Guru: It is his fate.

M: You have not assimilated the knowledge that I have been expounding. What is that *Ayurvedic* doctor doing? He wants to prolong that "I Amness" or Consciousness, which has appeared in that food-body.

(*The lady is talking in an irrelevant manner and everyone present tells Maharaj to ignore her.*)

You are not the personality or the individual. This body is the food-body on which Consciousness appears. The vital breath does all the work and Consciousness witnesses it all. This body is only the food-body for the consumption and the sustenance of the "I Amness." You have to remain in that Beingness or Consciousness with firm faith while having no identification with the body or the personality, or with name and form. Always identify yourself with Consciousness. It will take a while for this conviction to take root, but persist.

This Consciousness, which is there from childhood, prevails continuously till the vital breath leaves the body. Carry out all the activities in the objective world, but do not claim authorship for what is being done. As you begin to realize that all the activities are happening through you and that you are not doing anything, then gradually all your desires like the attachment for husband or wife, or greed for money, etc. will dwindle. All of that will go away once the sense of 'doership' disappears, because at that stage there will be no personality left to take credit for anything.

What thoughts are arising in you about these particular points?

Visiting Guru: If there is conviction in the "I Amness" or Beingness, then these questions will arise spontaneously. So where do these questions come from?

M: Where is the need for these questions if you are no longer an individual? If questions spring up, let them spring up. This body is there and this body is talking. It is not by any special desire that this body was created, or that everything is flowing – it happened spontaneously. So, why should I worry? As long as you are measuring everything in relation to your food-body, your relationship with this outer world is bound to be there, as well as your need to perform rituals or to achieve something. Once it is gone, you can no longer say you are a Hindu, Christian, or Buddhist. These are the traditions imposed on the body-mind. But since you are not the body-mind it is no longer valid.

Does your friend want to ask any questions?

V: This lady and I met in Dharamsala. We came here yesterday.

M: This body is not the yardstick for your identity. Is this principle getting confirmed in you? Whatever activities are happening are not individual but are a manifestation. As long as you are attached to your food-body you have to bear the consequences of physical actions. When you have detached from the body-consciousness and when whatever is done is offered or surrendered to *Brahman* or *Krishna*, you will be free from the results of all activity. Are there anymore explanations needed?

V: The ego is very strong.

M: As long as you are identifying with the body you are going to have the problem of the ego. If floods come and destroy some villages you cannot take credit or discredit for it. Similarly, you are not responsible for whatever is happening in nature's own course. You have a limited existence for a limited time. Once that limit is over you will merge with the Absolute (*Parabrahma*) and be gone. Once the vital breath has ceased, you no longer exist. Where is the truth of your Being? All this furious activity to achieve something is only the truth within the illusion. All of this was always an illusion. Presently you feel that 'You are'; this is a sort of reality but will only be there for a limited time.

Without the body
there is no "I Amness"

Maharaj: Who is he who is experiencing the illusion? Can he see himself? What identity do you give him?

Visitor: None other than the "I Am."

M: "I Am" is there without saying "I Am," do you agree? Are there any other points that you are not able to understand?

V: Sometimes, it seems that there are powers in the universe that lead me to wherever I should go. Why does it happen that way?

M: Activities take place because of the three *Gunas* (*Sattva*, *Rajas*, and *Tamas*), the five elements, the *Purusha* (the observer), and the *Prakriti* (the dynamic quality or *maya*). All activity is due to these ten aspects which arise from your Beingness.

There was a gentleman called Terence Stamp who was here for a few days. He was a very intelligent man and a great thinker. It is a pleasure to talk to such people, as it is mutually enjoyable and beneficial for both. The people who just listen and blindly follow should not come here. If they are unable to understand my knowledge they should recite *japa* instead. If the disciple repeats the sacred words, *"I am Brahman,"* that identity of *Brahman* will eventually sprout and manifest. Only then will that person be worthy to listen to my talks, and mature enough to understand what I am telling him.

V: Is 'love' the source of "I Am" or is "I Am" the source of 'love'? What is the relationship, if any, between love and hate and what are their sources?

M: "I Amness," Awareness without thought, is love. Love is not taken from "I Amness." The Self becomes manifest when love gets established as the "I Amness." When love starts loving the love, that is the Self. When everything is love there is no place for hatred. Only when the burning end of the incense stick hurts me do I get angry and throw it away. But if everything is Me, there is no question of hate.

V: If "I Amness" exists separate from the body, 'who' experiences the reaction from the incense stick?

M: The "I Amness" *is* because of the body. Without the body there is no "I Amness."

V: *What happens to the "I Amness" when the body falls down?*

M: The "I Amness," together with the vital breath, appear spontaneously when the body is created. The vital breath and the food-body are necessary to sustain the "I Amness." When the food-body is dropped by the vital breath, the "I Amness" disappears.

V: *Where does the "I Amness" go?*

M: Where does this flame go when it gets extinguished?

V: *Everywhere and nowhere.*

M: The same thing applies to the "I Amness."

V: *Does this teaching incorporate the reincarnation idea and does the "I Amness" reincarnate?*

M: So long as one identifies with the body and mind, one should think it so (*laughter*).

V: *Thank you, quite appropriate.*

M: These are all merely ideas. A villager who is afraid of ghosts and spirits will be afraid to walk alone at night, in case the spirits attack him. But a soldier who does not believe in spirits will not be afraid to walk alone in the forest at night. The ignorant, who are attached to their bodies, will be bound by concepts like reincarnation, whereas the man of understanding will have no fears about death or rebirth. *Jnana* is the knowledge; "I Amness" and *maya* are the watcher and the *lila*, respectively. The "I Am" is not involved in any of the activity. I am expounding this knowledge from the "I Am" level, though my normal state observes the "I Amness."

V: If the "I Am" concept tends to colour our experience, how can we tell how our experiences would be without that concept?

M: When you get established in the Beingness there are no thoughts or words – *You* are everything and everything is *You*. Later, even that ceases to exist.

Krishna made Arjuna realize that the whole world is *Krishna*. He realized that the knowledge "I Am," which means the manifestation of the entire universe, spontaneously appeared in him. Those couplets appear to have been taken from the Upanishads. They are identical. Whatever verses are produced in the Gita are part of the Mahabharata. The whole Gita section was not written by *Krishna*, but was a dictation by Sanjeya who was sitting in the palace telling Arjuna's enemies all that *Krishna* was saying. He had the power to see what was happening many miles away, and reproduced everything *Krishna* told Arjuna on the battlefield. Finally, Vyasa edited it all and put it across in the Mahabharata.

I talked to Maurice Frydman some four years back and he edited my words, emphasizing certain points and adding his own ideas, in the book 'I Am That'. That book and whatever was expounded at that time was only relevant for that period. I am speaking differently today. As a matter of fact, this should also have been recorded and published as it is in greater detail, and is emphasizing different aspects.

Without "I Amness" the Absolute does not know 'It is'

Maharaj: After being initiated by my Guru I used to discuss any doubts with my colleagues and *Gurubandhu* (Guru brothers). One day I mentioned a particular doubt to a friend. During one of our Guru's talks, my friend put across my question to the Guru. The Guru enquired whose doubt it was, and my friend replied, *"It is Maharaj's."* Our Guru suddenly sprang up and said, *"What, a doubt for you?"* He did not say anything more about it, but from that moment if ever a doubt appeared the answer would also appear.

Intuition comes according to the person sitting in front of me. Suppose there is someone sitting here. I may not ask him any questions directly, but may put a question to someone else instead. He may be stimulating questions in the other without even knowing it. I can tell people's state from their faces but I may not express it, because if they are at a lower level they could be offended.

Visitor: Did you say to be aware for twenty-four hours?

M: If you are encountering such a situation it is because you still identify yourself with the body-mind, and from that body-mind you want to merge with the "I Amness."

The dream world is the creation of your Consciousness and is created because of your Consciousness. It is the child of your Consciousness. Where is the question of you trying to merge again with Consciousness?

V: I think her question is that she would rather be without thoughts during the day, but in dreams she is not so aware of her body-mind. That is why she gets a little confused.

M: Whatever you do in the waking state, such as trying to get rid of your ego or to be without thoughts, will be repeated in the dream state. Instead, you have to come to that state where everything merges in your own Beingness. Then, since everything is already merged with Beingness, when that Beingness finally disappears everything will disappear along with it. That is the final state. Presently I am seeing this world due to the bright sunlight. But if a heavy cloud were to suddenly appear and block the sun, everything would disappear. This creation is without a womb. Similarly, this world in the waking state is created without a womb. There is no conception, no delivery, and no creation. The individual consciousness is working during the waking state.

When you go to sleep you think that consciousness also goes to sleep, but the Universal Consciousness is working even when you are asleep. It is the individual consciousness in the personality that goes to sleep. Therefore, the personality does not realize that the Universal Consciousness is still working, or that the entire universe is always working.

V: Is it the Universal Consciousness or the individual consciousness that creates?

M: These questions arise because of the conditioning of egoism. When you are in the "I Amness" there is no egoism – it is completely liquidated. Consciousness appears, is seen, and then again is gone. It is like the air in the sky. The mistake happens because we consider 'That' Consciousness to be the individual consciousness. 'Consciousness' means Universal Consciousness. In deep sleep the individual consciousness or personality forgets itself, but the universal action still goes on. Whatever you meditate on or think about before going to sleep, that process continues. That is why importance is given to the recitation of a sacred *mantra* just at the point of falling asleep – in order for that process to continue.

V: Does the "I Amness" without ego create Consciousness?

M: "I Amness" is without ego. The subsequent products are the mind and the ego.

V: Where does intuition come into this and how does it arise?

M: The quality of "I Amness" or Beingness *is* intuition and inspiration. Just like when you have a seed and plant it, it must sprout. Similarly, the quality of Beingness must sprout.

V: People are too lost in body-mind consciousness, to even consider Beingness. That is why I am asking about intuition.

M: Whatever identity a person holds on to, the quality of inspiration will be according to that.

V: Does the state of mind before we go to sleep affect our dreams?

M: Yes. Recite the sacred *mantra* and you will become established in the meaning of the *mantra*. Don't ask me questions from the standpoint of a human being, personality, or individual. Ask questions with the understanding that you are not an individual; identify instead with Consciousness or "I Amness."

V: We are not used to the sounds of the mantra. We need the words, but the meaning is not as great as when we say it in our mother tongue.

M: You can say both. You are a teacher and I want to talk to you.

V: From what I can see, the mind is that which maintains that separateness which we call reality. Before "I am That," "I Am."

M: You are giving all the importance to the mind, and think the mind is making all the difference.

V: "I Am" comes first.

Interpreter: In "I Am" there is no mind.

V: So "I Am" must be the source of the mind.

Interpreter: Yes, the mind springs up after "I Amness," but this "I Amness" is observed by the Absolute together with all of that action.

M: Yesterday we spoke about the two parts of the incense stick, the top end being the spark full of activity and the other end that is still and watching. The active part is called *maya*, and is due to the mind. The inactive part is the "I Amness," or *Purusha*, which is just watching. Only when you identify with that which is stationary, the *Purusha*, can you become the watcher of the "I Amness" and all of its activities. Without this "I Amness," the Absolute does not know that 'It is'. Watching is not deliberate. Watching happens to the Absolute only with the appearance of the "I Amness." The "I Amness," like binoculars, must be there and available for watching to happen.

V: If you are suggesting a position as the watcher, does it make any difference what the activities are? How does choice relate to that, if at all?

M: Whatever activities happen, happen only because of your "I Amness." They make no impression on that "I Amness." Judgements like good and bad are aspects of the mind, but if you are one with that "I Amness" then at that stage the mind is not there.

V: *This Universal Consciousness which you speak about, is it the same as the inner Guru or Satguru?*

M: If you are talking from the standpoint of a body-mind, an individual, or a human being, then you are going to compare *Satguru* with that Universal Consciousness. But if you become That, from the Absolute standpoint everything is One.

Ishwara means the expression of all form

Visitor: Meditation is not yet smooth for me. It feels bumpy.

Maharaj: The ideas that you are not stable and that it is bumpy are only ideas in your mind, and can only be captured by the mind.

V: Yes, that is why I am holding on firmly to the Witness.

M: Why be firm? Just be relaxed and question why there is effort.

V: Every moment is like amrit (nectar). It's very important to me and brings up the sense of effort rather than relaxing.

M: What is this effort you are doing in this moment that is like *amrit*?

V: I am making every effort of not being in the ego, or in the body-mind.

M: Where is the necessity of getting involved with the body?

V: *It is just a habit of all the past conditioning.*

M: Can a moment be nectar? A moment is a fragment of time. *Amrit* is eternity.

V: *If the "I Am" stays right in this moment, is it eternity?*

M: All of the moments are like sparks flying, but the Self is continuous.

V: *I am experiencing the "I Amness" a lot these days.*

M: Who is experiencing it? You *are* the Consciousness. There is no question of experiencing anything. Whatever is, is what *You* are. You are creating a separate identity.

V: *Yes, separation.*

M: The witnessing of the *Ishwara* state occurs to Me. *Ishwara* is the manifestation of the five elements and the universe. The witnessing of the "I Amness" occurs to the Absolute. A disciple (*sadhaka*) who is getting established in the *Ishwara* principle should not claim this understanding (*siddha*).

V: *Last night there was an* experience (*here I go again*) *of the "I Am" vibrating, like there was no body. It was very intense.*

M: In what form did you see that pulsation?

V: There was no form and no body. Something was forcing me to sit still and let it flow.

M: Whatever feeling or vibration you are having is only the product of the five elements.

V: Is it not the vital breath or the state of "I Amness?"

M: In addition to the five elements there are the three *Gunas* (types of behavioural qualities), the *Purusha* (the masculine principle), and the *Prakriti* (the feminine principle). These ten facets are the expression of your Beingness. My concept that *You* transcend the body-mind, which you accept, is for the kindergarten spiritual seeker. But now I am talking to the disciple who is already getting established in Beingness. So that first lesson should be over by now. The entire manifestation of your world and universe is just the expression and manifestation of your Beingness. The Consciousness, or *Ishwara*, is not that of an individual. *Ishwara* means the expression of all form.

Now you are listening to what I am saying. When you leave this place and talk to other people, you will say that Maharaj talked a lot and added even more confusion.

V: Not at all, the only thing happening is that it is so clear and fast. Besides, there is no place else to go.

M: This *Brahman* (or *Ishwara*) and this manifestation are Self-created, but within that you are there trying to modify things.

V: *The Consciousness senses that it is everything, that it is Ishwara. Then some desire spontaneously arises to modify or adjust things, and at that moment everything else happens and you realize you cannot adjust it, 'It is'.*

M: This will happen continuously, but you are not involved in that. *You* are aloof from that.

V: *That is why it is so helpful for me to be here.*

M: In spite of that, Delhi and the world are still far off! This chemical, this ingredient, is your "I Amness," and it is sustained by consuming this food-body. The Absolute is watching this "I Amness" that is sustained by the food-body. Is it clear? After some time passes in the waking state rest is required, so the "I Amness" goes into oblivion. It goes to rest and forgets itself. You may not comprehend exactly what it means now, but as you get established in Beingness you will understand how *You* are above the waking and dreaming states, because those are only expressions of your Beingness. The waking and dreaming states pertain only to your "I Amness." We are only able to observe because of the "I Amness." When the "I Amness" is not there, the tool to observe is also not there.

What happens is that while listening to what I am saying you are still entertaining some ideas about Consciousness. If my words tally with your concepts you are happy. But I want to blast all concepts and establish you in a 'no concept state'. Our prime minister, Morarji Desai, has got some firm ideas about God that he does not want to change. A lady who comes here knows the prime minister and gave him and his brother two books of my talks. Morarji just scanned through those books and said, *"I don't agree with this."* "I don't agree" means, "it does not tally with my concepts so I cannot accept it." He did not want his concepts to be blasted, but his brother was wonderstruck and said, *"There is some sense in this."*

V: So it's like, if I am deep inside then it's all gone and there is no "I Am?"

M: This "I Amness" merges in the Absolute.

Glossary

Ayurveda Ancient Indian science of life

Ayurvedic Pertaining to ayurveda

Brahma One of the Hindu trinity – the creator of the universe

Brahman The Absolute, the Ultimate Reality

dharma Code of conduct

ghee Clarified butter

Ishwara God

Krishna Avatar of Lord Vishnu

Mahasamadhi Death of a spiritual preceptor

mantra Sacred chant

mula-maya Primary illusion

Paramatma Supreme soul

pujya Highly respected

Rama Avatar of Vishnu and hero of Ramayana

samadhi One of the final stages of meditation; Oneness

Satguru True master

Shankara Another name of Shiva

Shiva One of the Hindu Trinity. God of destruction

Shiva Shakti Male and female cosmic energy. Shiva is the masculine, transcendent, eternal energy, and Shakti is the feminine, active, temporal energy

Veda A large corpus of texts originating in ancient India – the oldest scriptural texts of Hinduism

Vishnu One of the Hindu Trinity. Famed as the protector and rescuer.

yoga Union of the individualized consciousness with the Absolute, through the systematic practice of meditation, based on the eight-fold path prescribed by the ancient Sage Patanjali

yogi Anyone who practices yoga as a method of divine realization, whether he or she is a renunciate or a householder

yogic To do with yoga

For further details, contact:
Yogi Impressions Books Pvt. Ltd.
1711, Centre 1, World Trade Centre,
Cuffe Parade, Mumbai 400 005, India.

Fill in the Mailing List form on our website
and receive, via email, information on
books, authors, events and more.
Visit: www.yogiimpressions.com

Telephone: (022) 61541500, 61541541
E-mail: yogi@yogiimpressions.com

 Join us on Facebook:
www.facebook.com/yogiimpressions

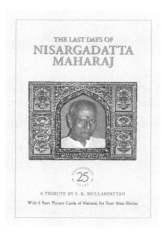

The Sacred India Tarot
Inspired by Indian Mythology and Epics
78 cards + 4 bonus cards + 350 page handbook
The Sacred India Tarot is truly an offering from India to the world. It is the first and only Tarot deck that works solely within the parameters of sacred Indian mythology – almost the world's only living mythology today.

Create greater balance and wholeness within yourself with

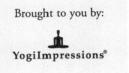

synchr⬤nicity®
Contemporary High-Tech Meditation® Audio CDs

When meditation was first conceived thousands of years ago, its techniques were suited for a simple, very different way of life. Today, we live in a chaotic, high-stress environment where time, calm and clarity can be elusive.

The Synchronicity Experience: quite simply, it meditates you
Its proprietary Holodynamic® Vibrational Entrainment Technology (HVET) developed by its Founder, Master Charles Cannon, is embedded in musical meditation soundtracks that literally meditate you while you listen.

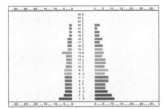
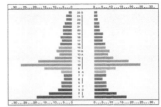

Brain monitor of a typical non-meditator shows pronounced hemispheric imbalance and fragmented, limited brain function.

A regular user of Synchronicity Contemporary High-Tech Meditation® develops a high degree of synchronization indicating whole brain function.

Taking the guesswork and randomness out of the meditative process, the meditation soundtracks are available in the Alpha and Theta formats for light and medium meditation. Whether you are an experienced meditator or just starting to meditate, our CDs will help deliver a four-fold increase in results compared to traditional methods.

| Om | Om Namah Shivaya | Harmonic Coherence | Welcome To My World | Om Mani Padme Hum |

Sounds Of Source Vol. 1-5   Time Off   Song Of The Ecstatic   Romancing The Moment The Love Meditation   Blessed Mother A Thousand Names

Hear the Audio Clips on our website: www.yogiimpressions.com